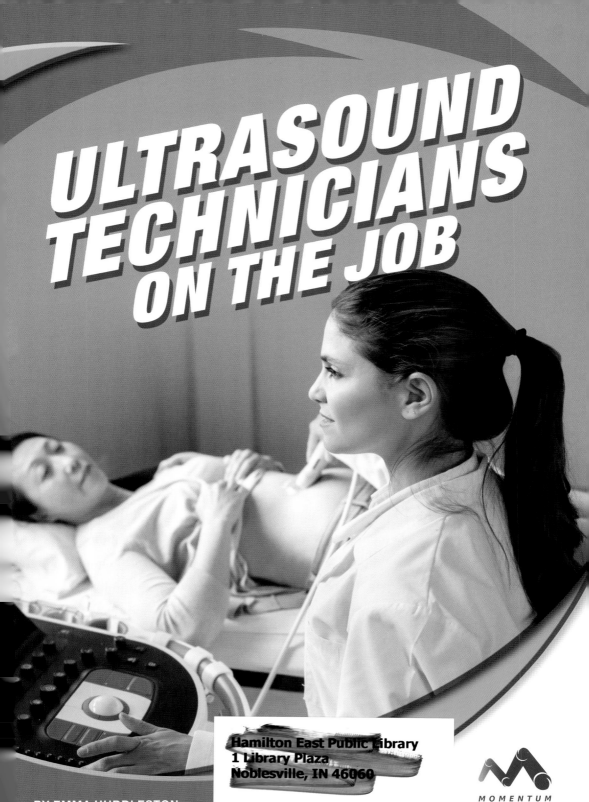

ULTRASOUND TECHNICIANS ON THE JOB

BY EMMA HUDDLESTON

MOMENTUM

Published by The Child's World®
1980 Lookout Drive • Mankato, MN 56003-1705
800-599-READ • www.childsworld.com

Content Consultant: Nikki Nordby, Registered
Diagnostic Medical Sonographer

Photographs ©: iStockphoto, cover, 1, 6, 9, 15, 25
(computer screen), 28; Monkey Business Images/
Shutterstock Images, 5, 12; J. Smith/iStockphoto,
10; Dmytro Zinkevych/Shutterstock Images, 13;
Shutterstock Images, 16, 19, 24, 26; Serhii Bobyk/
Shutterstock Images, 20; Monkey Business
Images/iStockphoto, 23; Myroslava Malovana/
Shutterstock Images, 25

ISBN 9781503835535
LCCN 2019943073

Printed in the United States of America

CONTENTS

MOMENTUM

FAST FACTS

What's the Job?

► Ultrasound technicians are also known as diagnostic medical sonographers. They use special technology to create images of inside the body, or they perform tests. Ultrasound techs give doctors these images and test results. The images and test results help doctors **diagnose** patients with problems or illnesses.

► Some people get a two- or four-year degree in sonography.

► Vascular sonography is a specialty. It focuses on the blood vessels and blood flow throughout the body. Some ultrasound clinics are made just for vascular sonography.

Important Stats

► In 2018, approximately 71,130 people worked as ultrasound techs in the United States.

► By 2026, the job for ultrasound techs is expected to grow by 23 percent.

► In 2018, the average salary for ultrasound techs was $73,860.

More than one-half of ultrasound techs ► work in hospitals. Others work in doctors' offices or medical laboratories.

CHAPTER ONE

BECOMING AN ULTRASOUND TECH

A lly walked quickly to class. She passed other students on the sidewalk. Her yellow notebook and heavy textbook bounced in her backpack. Ally was studying at the Cambridge Institute of Allied Health in Georgia. It was one of the best schools in the United States for ultrasound technicians. As Ally walked down the hallway, she remembered the day she knew she wanted to be an ultrasound tech.

In high school, Ally went with her mom to the doctor. Her mom was pregnant and got a sonogram at the appointment. The image was made using ultrasound technology. At first, the black and white sonogram looked blurry to Ally. The ultrasound tech explained what the image showed. Two gray lines were the baby's arms. A white spot was the baby's head. After the appointment, Ally wanted to learn how to use the technology.

◄ **People have to study hard and pay attention in class if they want to become an ultrasound tech.**

She could help people like her mom see what was happening inside their bodies.

Ally snapped out of her memory as class started. Today, they were learning about organs in the digestive system such as the stomach and liver. When class was over, Ally walked to the library. It was very quiet, which was good. She needed to study **anatomy**. She learned about bones, muscles, and parts of the body. It was an important class for ultrasound techs. Ally was getting an associate's degree. It would take her a little more than two years.

Besides going to class, Ally also spent time at the hospital. She got hands-on experience working with ultrasound techs. One of her first tasks was learning how to clean the equipment. Now, she was practicing how to use the ultrasound machine. The machine works by sending **high-frequency** sound waves into the body. The sound waves bounce off of organs and tissues. When they bounce, they create electrical signals. The signals are sent to a computer connected to the machine. It uses the signals to create an image of the organs and tissues.

All the ultrasound techs at the hospital were **certified**. This meant they took a test to prove their skills. Many were certified in more than one specialty. Ally didn't have to be certified to get a job. She could pass her test soon after getting hired.

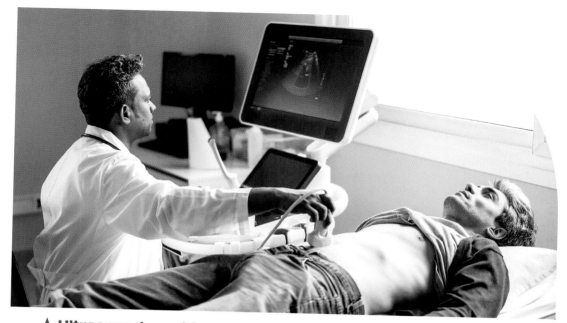

▲ **Ultrasound machines can be used for many reasons, such as looking for gallbladder disease and checking blood flow.**

But most employers looked for certification when they were hiring. For this reason, Ally wanted to be ready. After she graduated, she would take the test.

One day at the hospital, Ally was getting buttons on the ultrasound machine mixed up. She didn't remember how to change the frequency of the signals. She was frustrated. Millions of sound waves and signals were sent and received every second. One of the ultrasound techs at the hospital reminded her that it takes time to get used to doing ultrasounds. Not only does the machine have lots of parts, but every patient is different. They have different body sizes and shapes. Ally felt better after talking to the ultrasound tech. She tried again until she got it right.

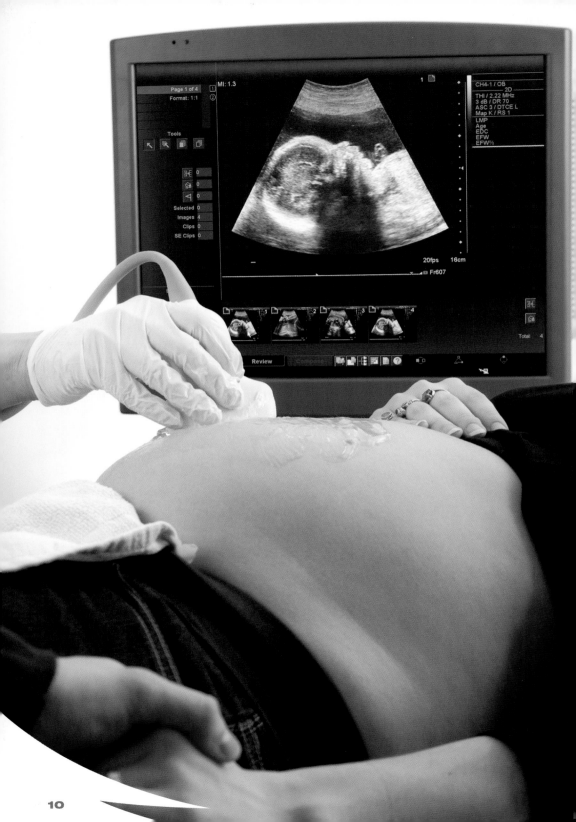

CHAPTER TWO

BABY ON THE WAY

Bright morning sunlight reflected off of the cars in the parking lot. Jen slid her own vehicle into an open space. In front of her was a brick building. It was a doctor's office where she was doing her internship. An internship is training experience to prepare for a specific job. Ultrasound tech internships could last three to six months. As an intern, Jen worked side-by-side with Barb, an experienced ultrasound tech.

Jen walked into the office. Barb was already talking to a female patient. Barb waved at Jen to follow them down the hallway. The woman was pregnant. She was here for her first ultrasound. Jen opened the exam room door. The ultrasound machine hummed quietly. The lights were dim. Sometimes this helped people relax. The woman laid back on the table. Barb sat at the ultrasound machine, and Jen stood next to her.

◄ **Ultrasounds allow parents to see their developing child.**

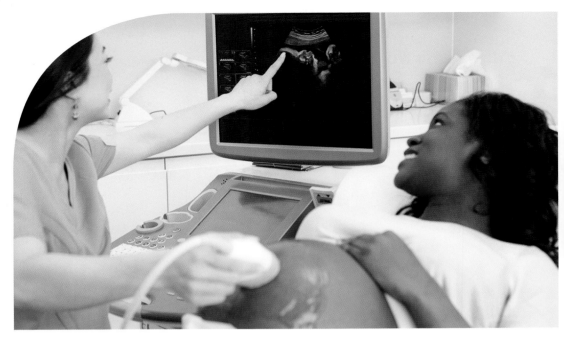

▲ **When a woman is further along in her pregnancy, ultrasounds can be used to check how healthy the baby is.**

Jen watched Barb multitask. Barb used her left hand to type. Her right hand moved the transducer across the woman's belly. The transducer is the small handheld piece connected to the machine by a cord. It is the part that touches the patient's body and sends sound waves inside.

Jen watched the computer screen. First, they looked to see if there was one baby or multiple babies. There was one. Barb turned the screen so the woman could see it. Barb pointed at the image. She explained where the baby was. Barb clicked buttons and moved the computer mouse. She measured the size of the baby. This would help them figure out when it would be born.

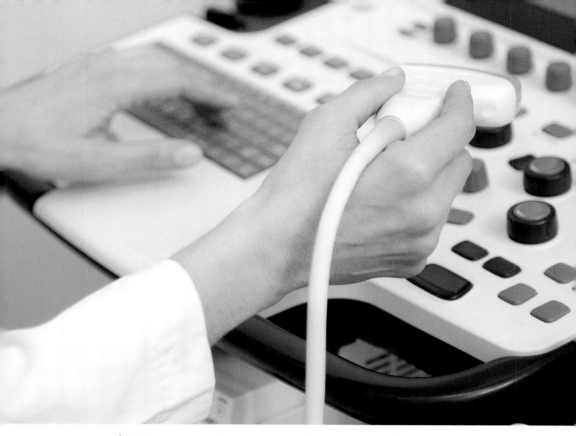

▲ **Ultrasound techs need to be familiar with how an ultrasound machine works.**

After the ultrasound, Jen helped schedule the woman's next appointment. She also updated the woman's patient files.

A few weeks later, Jen's internship was over. She was hired at the clinic as an ultrasound technician. Her specialty was obstetric sonography. That specialty focuses on pregnant women and their unborn babies. The images track the babies' health and growth. They also help watch for **birth defects**.

A few months later when Jen came into work for the day, she picked up her schedule. Her first appointment was with the pregnant woman she and Barb had helped when Jen was an intern. This time, Jen would do the woman's ultrasound on her own. A few minutes later, the woman arrived. Jen led her down the hall.

Jen's hand-eye coordination had improved during her internship. Doing multiple things at once was easier now. She took three measurements of the baby. She measured around its head and body. Then she measured the length of its leg. This data would tell them if it was growing properly. She also looked at the amount of fluid around the baby. The fluid gave it cushion and support. This time, Jen could see if it was a boy or girl. The woman wanted to know the baby's sex. Jen told the woman she was having a boy, and the woman smiled.

**Images of the baby can be given to ▶
parents after an ultrasound.**

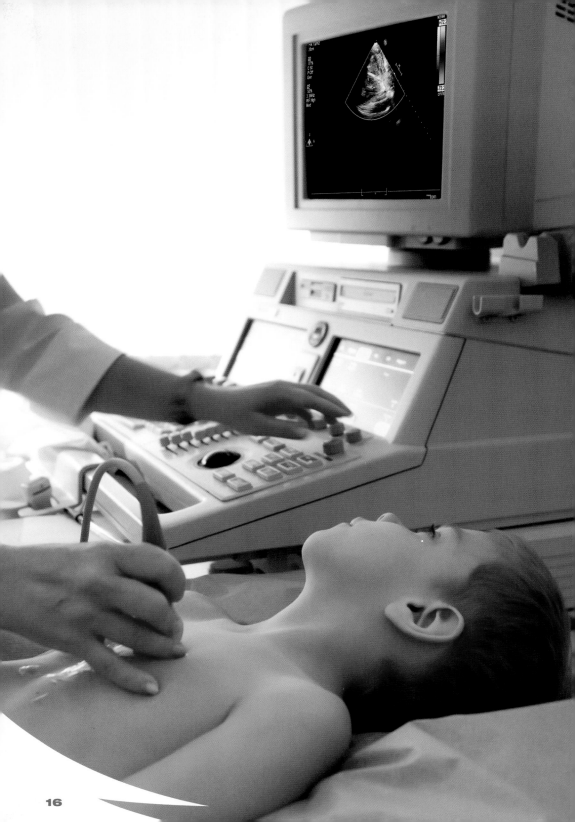

CHAPTER THREE

HEART PATIENTS

Norm poured two glasses of orange juice. One was for him, and one was for his daughter. Toast popped up from the toaster. He brought the juice, toast, butter, and strawberry jam to the table. They ate together before Norm left for work. He was an ultrasound tech with a specialty in cardiology. Cardiology is the study of the heart. It is an important field in countries like the United States because millions of older people live there. Blood clots and heart disease are common issues in older patients. Ultrasounds can safely and easily diagnose those issues.

At work, Norm saw several patients. One was an older man. He'd had a heart attack years ago. Now, he got regular ultrasounds to check on his heart. Norm got images of all parts of his heart. He looked for blocked arteries and blood clots. He used a special transducer. It was small and used low-frequency waves.

◄ **Sometimes, young children need ultrasounds on their hearts.**

It could calculate how fast an object was moving. It is often used to measure blood flow through the heart. When an object moves toward the transducer, the echoes are high frequency. As the object moves away, the frequency becomes lower.

Norm knew the man was nervous. He did not want any more heart issues. Norm smiled after the ultrasound and told him the first half of the appointment was done. He wiped down the machine while the patient put his shirt back on. Then, Norm led him to another room. This was to complete a special test. Many heart patients did **EKG** testing. EKG testing monitors a patient's heart during exercise to see how it handles stress.

First, Norm attached sticky pads to the man's chest, arms, and legs. They would send and receive electric signals. Then, he turned on a treadmill. The man walked on the treadmill for exercise. Norm watched the computer. The screen showed a thin line tracing the patient's heartbeats. It spiked up and down. The spikes were closer together as the patient's heart rate got faster. After the test, Norm removed the pads and gave the patient a cup of water. He was done with testing. Norm put the ultrasound image and EKG test in the man's patient files.

Norm met with the man's doctor and gave her a summary of the patient's tests. This kept the doctor up to date in case the man had issues. The man's tests showed his heart was healthy.

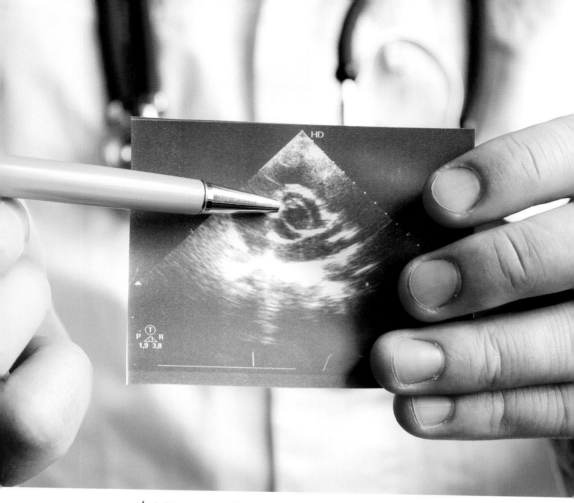

▲ **Ultrasounds let doctors know how the heart is functioning.**

When he got home that night, Norm and his daughter decided to watch a movie. But Norm made sure he didn't stay up too late. He had another busy day at work ahead. When Norm woke up the next morning, his daughter surprised him with breakfast. She brought him a glass of orange juice and a slice of toast. Norm smiled. He felt rested and ready for another day of work.

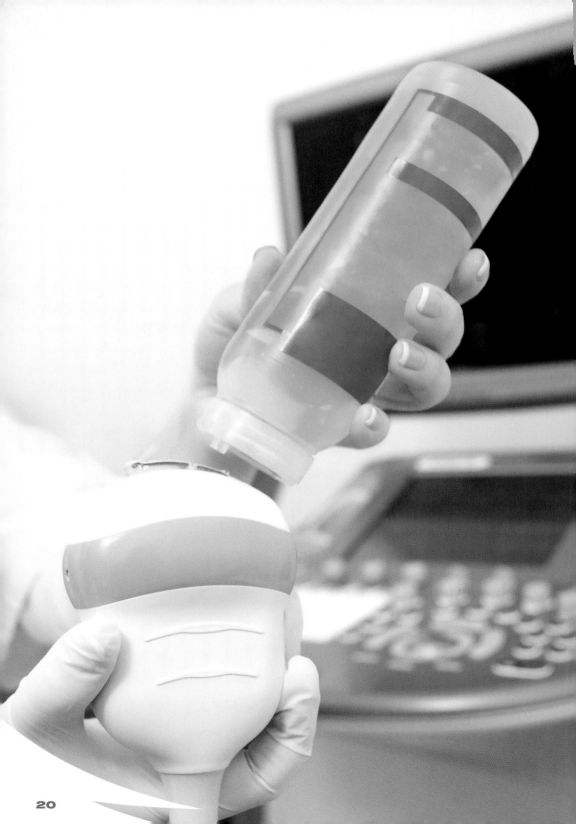

CHAPTER FOUR

BREAST CANCER

W hen Maya woke up, sunlight was streaming through her windows. The big oak tree in her front yard was shedding its red leaves. It was October, which was Breast Cancer Awareness Month. Hundreds of thousands of women die from breast cancer each year. Maya's mother died of it when Maya was young. That was the main reason Maya became an ultrasound tech. She wanted to help diagnose breast cancer so women could get help before it was too late.

A picture of Maya's mom hung on the fridge. It was faded and old. She saw it as she walked out the door. She drove to the hospital. She had been working there for more than 25 years. Many ultrasound techs work at hospitals. Sometimes, Maya worked odd hours because hospitals were open at all times. But Maya didn't mind. She was used to it after such a long career.

◀ **Ultrasound gel helps improve the quality of an image.**

Maya knew most of the employees at the hospital. They smiled at her and said good morning. Maya was known for her kindness and hard work. It was not easy seeing patients at the hospital. They could be sick or going through a difficult time. Later that day, Maya met a new patient. She came in because she found a lump in her breast. It could be a sign of breast cancer.

Before doing the ultrasound, Maya recorded the patient's medical history. This included asking questions about her age and past illnesses. Maya also asked if any of her family members had illnesses such as cancer.

The woman had recently had a **mammogram**. Her results showed she had dense breast tissue. Sometimes these results were early warning signs of cancer. An ultrasound could help diagnose whether her breast tissue was healthy. But she had never had an ultrasound before. Maya made sure to answer all of the patient's questions and explained the process. She showed the patient some blue gel and explained why it was used. The gel removes air between the transducer and the body. It lets sound waves pass into the body better.

Once she answered the patient's questions, Maya turned on a piece of equipment that would take an image of the woman's breast. The machine was great for early tumor detection.

**Mammograms are X-rays that can ▶
help detect breast cancer.**

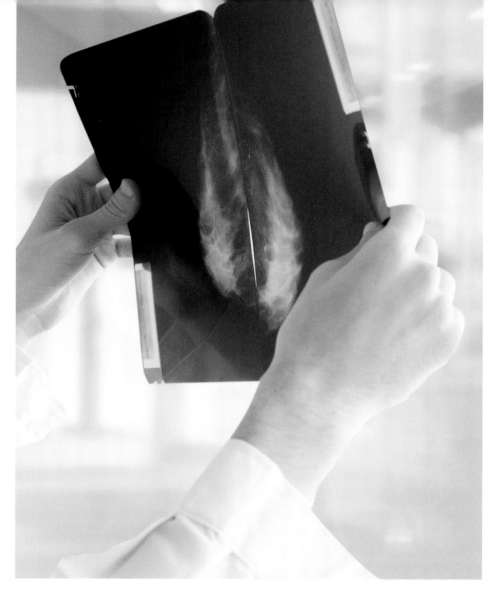

▲ **Medical professionals use imaging technology, such as mammograms, to see if there are any signs of a tumor.**

The image gave doctors a better look at the breast tissue. Maya watched the computer screen. She did not see anything abnormal. But she still sent them to the doctors for review.

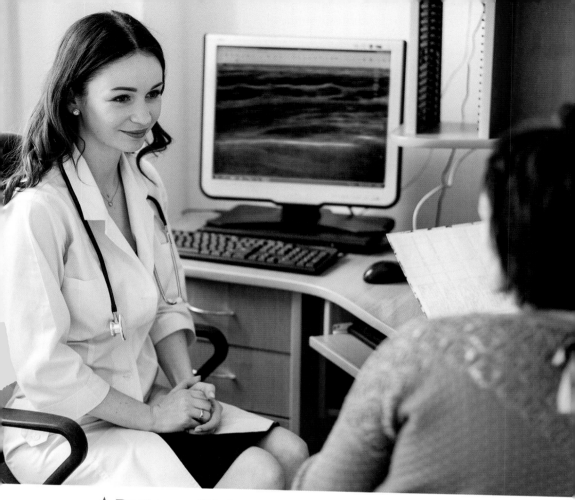

▲ **Doctors will let patients know if something doesn't look right in their ultrasound.**

Information like this helps doctors decide if treatment is needed and what options are best for the patient.

Maya shook the woman's hand on her way out of the room. She was the last patient for the day. When Maya got home, she thought about her mother. Maya was sad she was gone, but Maya was proud of the career she had picked.

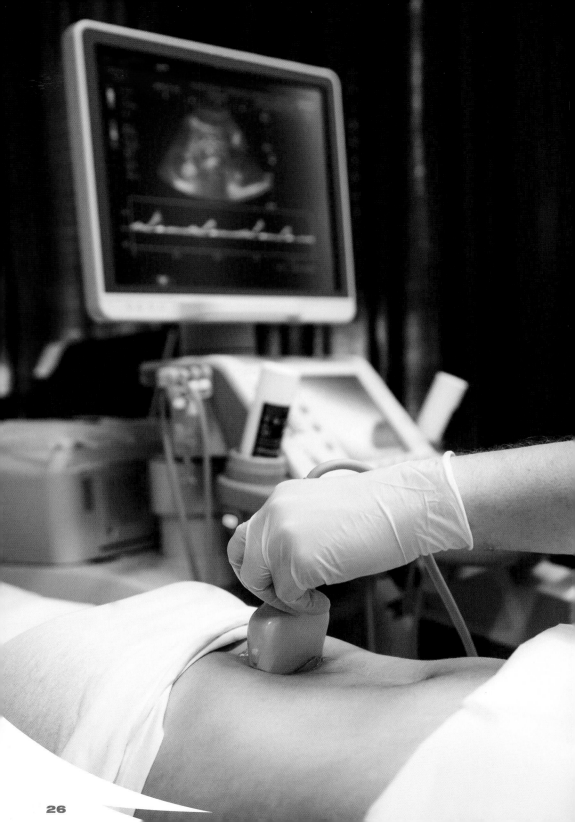

CHAPTER FIVE

A BUSY HOSPITAL

Wendy heard a phone ringing, people talking, and doors slamming shut. She was at the hospital, but she wasn't a patient. She was an ultrasound tech. She specialized in **abdominal** organs such as the liver, pancreas, and spleen. She chose that specialty because she thought abdominal organs were interesting. They were involved in many functions of the human body.

Sometimes, Wendy thought about each patient's situation as a mystery. She worked both on her own and as a team with doctors. Wendy helped gather information by doing ultrasounds. Then, she used her problem-solving skills with doctors to diagnose patients.

A man in the waiting room winced in pain. He felt sick and had abdominal cramps. Wendy showed him to an exam room.

◄ **Ultrasounds are usually the first kind of image test that medical professionals will use when they think a patient might have a disease.**

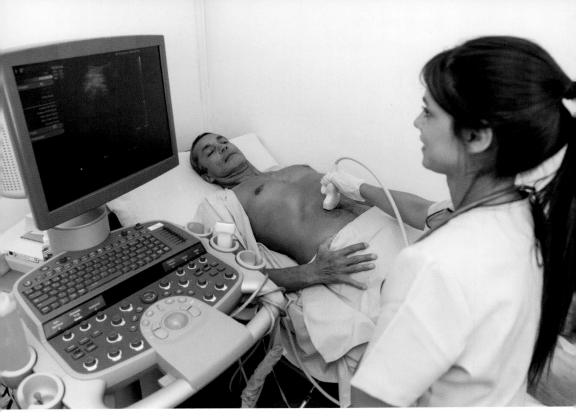

▲ **Ultrasound techs work hard to help patients.**

She looked at his file. It showed blood tests from a few days ago. The results were normal. So Wendy did an ultrasound.

The paper on the table crinkled under the patient's body as he laid down. He turned on his side so Wendy could get an image of his kidney. She found the problem. He had a kidney stone. Kidney stones are tiny crystals. Sometimes they are caused by eating too much salt and sugar. Those minerals can be hard for the kidney to process in large amounts. They stick together and form crystals that grow into a kidney stone.

Wendy pressed buttons on the keyboard. She zoomed in on the kidney stone. She measured it. It was small enough for him to pass. That meant the stone would eventually get out through the man's urine, but it might be painful. She explained that pain medication and drinking lots of water could help. Then the man left. She wrote a report and put it in his file. His case wasn't serious, so she didn't have to alert anyone about the issue.

Wendy wiped down the machine. She replaced the paper on the table. She threw away the plastic covering on the transducer. It had blue jelly on it. Finally, the room was clean. Wendy was ready for her next patient.

THINK ABOUT IT

► If you were an ultrasound tech, what specialty would you be interested in? Would you want to do images of hearts, babies, or abdominal organs? Explain your choice.
► Why are ultrasound techs important?
► Why is it important that ultrasound techs know how to use ultrasound machines?

GLOSSARY

abdominal (ab-DOM-uh-nul): The abdominal part of the body does not include the head, arms, or legs. An ultrasound of abdominal organs could show the liver.

anatomy (uh-NAT-uh-mee): Anatomy is the science of the body's structure and how it works. Ally studied anatomy to become an ultrasound tech.

birth defects (BURTH di-FEKTZ): Birth defects are problems that happen while the baby is developing in the mother's womb. Ultrasound images can be used to discover birth defects.

certified (SUR-tuh-fyed): People become certified after they pass a test proving they have specialized skills and knowledge. Ultrasound techs can become certified.

diagnose (dye-uhg-NOHS): To diagnose is to identify a sickness or the cause of a health problem. Doctors use information from ultrasound images to diagnose patients.

EKG: An EKG is a test that tracks a patient's heartbeat. Patients who are at risk for heart attacks often do EKG testing.

high frequency (HYE FREE-kwuhn-see): High frequency is when something occurs at a fast pace. Ultrasound machines use high-frequency waves to make images.

mammogram (MAM-uh-gram): A mammogram is an X-ray of a woman's breast. The doctor used a mammogram to determine whether a lump could be caused by a problem such as cancer.

TO LEARN MORE

BOOKS

Mooney, Carla. *Medical Technology and Engineering*.
Vero Beach, FL: Rourke Educational Media, 2012.

Wilcox, Christine. *Health Care Careers*.
San Diego, CA: ReferencePoint Press, 2019.

Wyskowski, Lindsay. *Life with Cancer*.
Mankato, MN: The Child's World, 2019.

WEBSITES

Visit our website for links about ultrasounds: **childsworld.com/links**

Note to Parents, Teachers, and Librarians: We routinely verify our Web links to make sure they are safe and active sites. So encourage your readers to check them out!

SELECTED BIBLIOGRAPHY

"Diagnostic Medical Sonographers." *Bureau of Labor Statistics*, 29 Mar. 2019, bls.gov. Accessed 4 June 2019.

"How & Why to Become a Certified Ultrasound Technician." *All Allied Health Schools*, n.d., allalliedhealthschools.com. Accessed 4 June 2019.

McKay, Down Rosenberg. "What Does an Ultrasound Technician Do?" *Balance Careers*, 23 Apr. 2019, thebalancecareers.com. Accessed 4 June 2019.

INDEX

ABOUT THE AUTHOR

Emma Huddleston lives in Minnesota with her husband. She enjoys writing children's books, but she likes reading novels even more. When she is not writing or reading, she likes to stay active by running, hiking, or swing dancing.